INSIDER HOLLYWOOD

Sally Whitehill

Colette House
52-55 Piccadilly
London W1J 0DX
United Kingdom

Email: info@bluffers.com
Website: bluffers.com
Twitter: @BluffersGuide

First published 2013

Publisher: Thomas Drewry
Publishing Director: Brooke McDonald

Series Editor: David Allsop
Design and Illustration: Jim Shannon

A CIP Catalogue record for this book is available from the British Library.

ISBN: 978-1-909365-16-2 (print)
978-1-909365-17-9 (ePub)
978-1-909365-18-6 (Kindle)

CONTENTS

Hollywood is a town where the phrase 'Fake it until you make it' is less of a cliché and more of a direct instruction for a desirable mode of living.

TRUE LIES IN TINSELTOWN

Living and working in Hollywood requires levels of optimism and inflated self-belief rarely seen outside Third World dictatorships, end-of-the-world cults, or investment banking.

The types of people who thrive in Hollywood are hustlers, scoundrels and egomaniacs. It is an industry built on chutzpah, hyperbole and downright lies. It is a town where the phrase: 'Fake it until you make it' is less of a cliché and more of a direct instruction for a desirable mode of living. Put simply, Hollywood is the ideal environment for bluffers.

All Hollywood veterans remember the feeling they had when they first bluffed their way into a gig. There was the flash of glory as they successfully pretended they knew more about the film and television industry than anyone else in the room – perhaps even the world – and, as a result, were given a disproportionate amount of power and responsibility.

Once welcomed inside Hollywood's golden halls, our brave bluffers discovered another truth. One sunny Los

Angeles day, while jauntily ascending from their golf cart to their personalised Star Wagon, they realised that everyone around them had done exactly the same thing. There were entire companies and film sets where no one knew what the hell they were doing. The place was rife with bluffers. They were everywhere, wafting through the ranks without lifting a finger.

This book will give you the tools you need to bluff about Hollywood and the entertainment industry. It will allow you to convince awestruck admirers that you have peeked into the closed sets of the studio backlots, flown with the stars on private jets, played poker with the moguls and had plastic surgery with their trophy wives (or husbands). All this, without ever having to reveal that the closest you've been to Hollywood is your local multiplex.

HOW IT ALL STARTED

There are many myths about the founding of Hollywood. Most of them are untrue, and in order for you to assert yourself as an expert in the field, it is helpful to be able to allude to some of the basics. So, feel free to assume an air of nonchalant indifference as you drop the following golden nuggets into conversation, with appropriate pauses for emphasis; these, of course, should not be long enough to open yourself up to questions.

That could be dangerous.

MOVIES ON THE RUN

Let's get straight to the point: Hollywood was founded by people on the run.

In the early twentieth century, movie companies in New York were dodging film-stock and camera manufacturers (aka 'The Trust') who wanted licence fees on each movie that had been made with their equipment. Accordingly, these manufacturers sent hired goons who could clear film sets faster than a mogul's wife could pillage Bergdorf Goodman. Demanding an exorbitant fee for something with which you had nothing to do is old hat in today's Hollywood, but back in the quaint 1920s, this was still seen as, well, a trifle pushy.

Desperate to escape The Trust's hoodlums (and perhaps also their own free-spending wives), some filmmakers began to explore new territories.

BRAVE EXPLORERS

One of the first brave explorers to the West Coast was director DW Griffith. Here, you may feel the need to wipe a tear from your eye (poignantly) as you recall how, in 1910, he set out for California alone – except for a troupe of actors – to change the course of movie history. He did this by shooting the first film ever made in Hollywood. It was called *In Old California,* and was a short film, which was probably for the best, as it wasn't very good.

There is a valuable lesson here to all bluffers about the importance of making a good first impression.

A couple of years later, director Cecil B DeMille and producer Jesse L Lasky also arrived in the Golden State. They had initially set out for Flagstaff, Arizona, but got off the train, looked around and got right back on again and stayed to the end of the line – which happened to be Los Angeles. Here they shot Hollywood's first full-length feature, *The Squaw Man.*

If Arizona hadn't been such a bummer, the course of moviemaking history might have been completely different. There is a valuable lesson here to all bluffers about the importance of making a good first impression.

THE FIRST BLUFF

The first Hollywood motion picture studio was founded in 1911. Two brothers from New Jersey, David and William Horsley, bought a decrepit pub on the corner of Sunset Boulevard and Gower Street. Not ones to be held back by appearances, they grandly named it 'The Nestor Motion Picture Company' (one wonders why they chose this particular character from Greek mythology, as Nestor was infamous for giving people bad advice in Homer's *Odyssey*). The founding of Nestor may have been the first Hollywood bluff – and it worked. A year later the brothers merged their company (renamed Nestor Studios) with Carl Laemmle* and other independent filmmakers to form the more prosaically named Universal Film Manufacturing Company.

*Bluffers should be cautious when discussing Carl Laemmle. The correct pronunciation of Mr Laemmle's name is *lem-lee*. Ogden Nash once referred to Laemmle's penchant for nepotism using verse: 'Uncle Carl Laemmle/Has a very large faemmle', which is a useful *aide-memoire* in any discourse about Hollywood history.

THE ARRIVAL OF THE MOGULS

Carl Laemmle

Laemmle was a shrewd businessman. In 1914, Universal bought 230 acres of land in the San Fernando Valley. This was a massive step up from the former boozer owned by the Horsley brothers. It was a megalopolis, able to produce up to 250 films, shorts and newsreels a year. Laemmle, with perhaps a little hubris, called this whole area 'Universal City'. He was keen to show off his new digs and, much to the chagrin of anyone actually trying to make a film, invited members of the general public to visit the lot.

Laemmle basically invented the idea of the theme park. Families worldwide have Uncle Carl to thank for endless days spent queuing for rides in the baking sun with the misguided belief that this is quality time that somehow bonds you all together, which it does – by mutual misery and despair.

Besides Laemmle, other moguls fled west around the same time. Any bluffer worth his or her salt should be able to reference the following rogues' gallery. (You will notice that many of them changed their names en route, and we thoroughly encourage this tactic.)

Harry Cohn (aka King Cohn)

Harry was the co-founder and president of Columbia Pictures. He described running a studio as 'better than being a pimp'. In later years, his love of aphorisms caught up with him when US comedy actor Red Skelton remarked of the crowds at Cohn's funeral: 'It proves what Harry always said: "Give the public what they want and they'll come out for it".'

Sam Goldwyn

Sam Goldwyn started life in Warsaw, Poland, as Schmuel Gelbfisz. When he moved to Birmingham, England, he changed his name to Samuel Goldfish in an effort to fit in with the natives. Sam's difficulties with the English language plagued him throughout his life, and he is reportedly responsible for such corkers as 'I don't think anybody should write his autobiography until after he's dead', 'In two words: Im Possible' (although Charlie Chaplin later took credit for that one), and 'The next time I send a damn fool for something, I go myself'. Yet Sam's malapropisms didn't stop him from becoming one of the most powerful men in Hollywood. He found fame chiefly as an independent producer. In a lesson to bluffers everywhere, he never produced a film with the studio that bore his name, Metro-Goldwyn-Mayer (MGM).

Louis B Mayer

'LB' (born Eliezer or Lazar Meir in Minsk, Belarus) started life in the junk business. Noting the similarities between this profession and Hollywood, he moved to LA, where he ran MGM. He also owned one of the best stables in America. He was known for his aptitude in dealing with stars and horses, possibly using techniques for training the latter on the former.

The Warner Brothers

Harry, Albert, Sam and Jack. Born to Polish immigrant parents from Ostrołęka, at home these brothers were also known as Hirsz, Aaron, Szmul and Itzhak Wonskolaser. Wisely, they decided to change their names when they emigrated, and one of the most successful studios of the twentieth century was born.

Darryl Zanuck

There are many accounts of the career of legendary mogul Darryl Zanuck. One of them is that his Hollywood path started at eight years of age, when he secured a role as an extra. 14 years later, he was back in town, this time as a writer of *Rin Tin Tin* scripts for Warner Bros. His relationship with Rinty, the affable German shepherd, opened doors for him and he ended up as head of Twentieth Century Fox. Despite his many successes, his relationship with the dog was arguably one of his most amicable, given his eventual resignation from Twentieth after a bitter power struggle. As Marilyn Monroe once opined: 'Dogs never bite me. Just humans.'

Adolph Zukor

Zukor was born Adolph Cukor in Hungary. He reportedly flirted with the idea of changing the first initial of his surname to an 'f', which may have resulted in an entirely different career (and certainly a mention in *The Bluffer's Guide to Sex*). His first job was as a furrier. He knew more than one way to skin a cat, however, and eventually ended up co-founding Paramount Pictures.

THE RISE OF THE STARS

In the early 1900s, the stars of films were not credited on screen. This changed when Carl Laemmle hired the poetically named Florence Lawrence. Florence was a Canadian actress who holds a place in the hearts of multitasking bluffers everywhere, having claimed to have invented the turn and brake signals for automobiles in between takes. Before 1910, Florence was simply known as the 'Biograph Girl'. Once Laemmle signed her, all this changed. He promoted Ms Lawrence, using her name – and the idea of the 'movie star' was born. So, too, was the idea of the 'outrageous salary'.

Unfortunately Florence's reign as queen of Hollywood was short-lived. She made a series of bad marriages and died in poverty in West Hollywood in 1938, having eaten ant poison.

YOU AIN'T HEARD NOTHIN' YET

Florence's bad luck with men was not the only reason for the demise of her career. Before the ink was dry on her second marriage certificate, Hollywood had already begun to look for a different kind of star. By the late 1920s, the 'talkies' were gaining popularity. Warner Bros' 1927 hit, *The Jazz Singer,* was the first full-length movie with synchronised dialogue sequences. It marked the beginning of the end of the silent movie era – and the demise of many of its actors' careers.

Oscar-winning flick *The Artist* is set in this period and is something you may want to insinuate that you have seen. In a nutshell: arrogant silent movie star meets beautiful wannabe starlet. He falls on hard times; her star rises. There's dancing, romance and, most importantly, a cute dog.

THE GOLDEN AGE OF HOLLYWOOD

The Jazz Singer was the start of the Golden Age of Hollywood. It was golden for the usual reason: people made loads of money. The talkies were a phenomenon, and people around the globe would trot off every week to enjoy the new wonders of technology and a squeeze in the back row of the cinema.

Studios began to churn out movies at an astounding rate. They were able to do this for a few reasons:

- They had contracts with writers, directors and stars that lasted for years, not just the duration of a single project. No need to engage in pesky negotiations that could stall the process of making studios yet more cash!
- They sold movies in 'blocks', flogging a year's worth of films to cinemas at a time. This meant that for every *Gone with the Wind,* cinemas would also be lumbered with an egregious *Plan 9 from Outer Space.*
- Complaints about the above were minimal – not least because the studios actually owned the cinemas, too.

The moguls had figured out a way to monopolise the film industry. They began to treat filmmaking like running a factory, with some pretty incredible results. For example, in one year alone, 1939, they released *The Wizard of Oz, Gone with the Wind, Stagecoach, Mr Smith Goes to*

Washington, Wuthering Heights, Only Angels Have Wings, Ninotchka and *Midnight.*

Of course, there is no need for you to have seen these films; a mere nod to their uncontested brilliance will be enough. If you fancy taking the bluff a little further, however, feel free to chuck in some of the following names: Garbo, Bogart, Bacall, Gable, Hepburn, Astaire, Rogers, Stewart, Keaton, Garland, Grant, Monroe. The use of surnames here will single you out as a serious student of film (or the alumnus of a rather stiff British public school).

THE DECLINE OF THE STUDIO SYSTEM

All good things must come to an end, and so, too, did Hollywood's Golden Age. The bewhiskered villain of its demise came in the form of Thurman Arnold. Like many moviegoers then and now, Mr Arnold was frustrated by some of the dross he was seeing at the cinema. But unlike many moviegoers, he happened to be US assistant attorney general from 1938-43 in charge of the antitrust division.

After enduring one too many stinkers at movie theatres, Arnold decided that enough was enough. This was a man with a last name as a first name, after all, and so history had already denoted that he must be a person of action. He launched a petition against block-booking and monopolisation of distribution.

Arnold was so effective that, by 1949, all the major studios had given up ownership of their cinemas – although to his disappointment, it didn't mean that all bad movies had stopped being produced.

THE AUTEURS, AKA THE AGE OF THE BLUFFERS

Emboldened by the French (funny how they're always close by when trouble starts), a new wave of Hollywood filmmakers seized power from the studios in the 1960s. They modelled themselves after their European cousins, the *auteurs* (definition [French]: 'author'; definition [American]: 'pain in a studio executive's ass'). Whenever you refer to the *auteurs* you should gaze dreamily into the middle distance and speak lovingly of Jean-Luc Godard and François Truffaut – in a perfect French accent, of course.

The *auteur* movement in the USA was a little more woolly than its French cousin. It is really more of a shorthand to describe a period in Hollywood when directors, writers and actors were given (or took) a far freer rein in filmmaking. This generation may also have been one of the most irresponsible cohorts of filmmakers ever to grace Hollywood. They drank heavily, they took drugs ('The cocaine problem in the United States is really because of me. There was no cocaine on the street before *Easy Rider*; after *Easy Rider*, it was everywhere,' said Dennis Hopper) and they bankrupted studios (*Heaven's Gate*/United Artists). It was like having a bunch of unruly children running amok, making grandiose claims about their abilities. Ethically, this is the generation many bluffers may identify with most.

The problem with this gang is that, while many of them may have been filthy, beardy druggies, they were really rather good at what they did. Warner Bros' *Bonnie and Clyde* from 1967 is the movie you should refer to as marking the beginning of the dominance of 'New Hollywood' by this bunch of young, noisy *arrivistes.*

Bonnie and Clyde was quickly followed by *The Graduate* (1967), *Easy Rider* (1969), *The Godfather* (1972), *American Graffiti* (1973), *The Exorcist* (1973), *Chinatown* (1974), *Jaws* (1975), *Taxi Driver* (1976), *Star Wars* (1977) and *Apocalypse Now* (1979).

THE 1980s AND 1990s: BLOCKBUSTERS AND THE RISE OF THE HOME VIDEO MARKET

The kids of the 1960s and 1970s may have believed in sex, drugs and rock 'n' roll, but they also held an abiding passion for something else: money. *The Godfather, Jaws* and *Star Wars,* with their annoyingly talented directors, could all have been ignored if they didn't have that one special gift that Hollywood prizes above all else: the ability to make money at the box office.

These movies turned the tide in Hollywood, making the 1980s and 1990s not just the decades of shell suits, bum bags and criminally bad perms, but also the years of the reinvented blockbuster, with movies such as *Raiders of the Lost Ark* (1981), *ET* (1982), *Ghostbusters* (1984), *Back to the Future* (1985), *Jurassic Park* (1993) and *Titanic* (1997).

The home video market also opened up in the 1980s. This had two results: it gave studios another market to exploit and created another arena in which to make huge profits.

THE PRESENT

Bluffing about the present state of Hollywood is where you can really come into your own. Although bluffers are not known to deal exclusively in facts, there are a couple you can refer to.

What is irrefutable is that the blockbuster is still around. There is also a thriving demand for comic books and sequels. And something called 'pre-brand awareness', which is when you buy something that other people know already, like a book, or a film about a social media giant (let's just hypothetically say Facebook) because you can't trust yourself to market an original idea.

When asked to put forward an opinion about the current state of Hollywood, you should stroke your chin thoughtfully and double-bluff your audience with this epithet from Academy Award-winning screenwriter and author William Goldman: 'Nobody knows anything.'

A well-timed wink will assure them that this, of course, doesn't apply to you.

EQUIPMENT

Besides an indefatigable sense of self-belief, there are some items of equipment that any respectable Hollywood bluffer could not do without. It is not only important to acquire these gadgets and gizmos, but to be able to give the impression that you have a working knowledge of how to use them.

PDAS

The PDA is the personal digital assistant, not the public display of affection (which in Hollywood is only used when: 1) there is a camera around, or 2) you are about to really shaft someone). All Hollywooders are glued to their BlackBerrys or iPhones. Some people have been known to have longer, more satisfying relationships with these gizmos than their actor/model/whatever other halves.

Many insiders find themselves afflicted with 'BlackBerry thumb': the workaday cousin of tennis elbow. They also have a chronically short attention span. Think of it this way: the BlackBerry is the electronic equivalent of having the postman ring your doorbell every 10 seconds. It's bound to drive anyone batty.

Phone calls and emails are part of the incessant forward thrust of Hollywood life. California passed legislation in 2008 prohibiting mobile phone use while driving, but that didn't stop anyone. Hollywood runs this state – not Sacramento. Now Hollywooders can be seen wildly gesticulating and yelling with futuristic *Robocop*-style devices inserted into their ears as they negotiate multimillion-dollar deals. The best ones give an uncanny impression of a schizophrenic off their meds, as they mutter, grimace and throw things, all the time seemingly speaking into thin air.

Occasionally throw in well-worn Hollywood epithets, such as 'Weinstein can kiss my ass!'

This makes life easier for any imposter. Not only do you not have to go to the trouble of finding someone to take your phone call, you don't even need a phone. Simply hold your hand to your ear, as if adjusting a particularly tight-fitting ear bud, then stridently pace along the streets of Beverly Hills shrieking about trailer size, car service and the private jet. Occasionally throw in well-worn Hollywood epithets, such as: 'Weinstein can kiss my ass!', 'There hasn't been a good Oscar-cast since the '80s' and 'Is Billy Crystal still *alive*?'

To adapt this practice for use in a car, simply raise your voice and wind the windows down so that others can hear you. For consummate bluffers, we suggest attaching a megaphone to the roof, as councillors do in rural elections, to ensure that no one misses a word you're saying.

CARS

As per the above, a lot of business can be done – or at least, can be seen to be done – on the road. Angelenos are notoriously bad drivers. They are so 'scheduled up the wazoo' (definition: noun. 'one's rear trapdoor') that they see car travel as another perfect multitasking opportunity. At any given time, on any highway in Los Angeles, they will be performing a combination of the following: applying make-up, drinking coffee, flossing, emailing, cleaning their ears, eating, watching television, negotiating a deal on the latest *Batman* franchise. All, of course, at 60mph.

Many of their vehicles, although expensive, are missing not entirely cosmetic external parts, such as wing-mirrors and bumpers. Others have mysterious scrapes and dents. This is the price of success in Hollywood, and you must embrace it.

Talk loudly to friends about the number of car accidents you caused in Los Angeles and the unfairness of the rear-end law in California. Hire the most expensive car you can find (be sure to take out all the insurance), then ram it with reckless abandon into walls, bollards and other cars.

When others see your misused vehicle, proudly tell them that it's a result of having learned to drive in Hollywood.

CLOTHES

Ever since *Pretty Woman,* everyone knows that the only difference between a hooker and a trophy wife is a pretty frock. Julia Roberts popped down Rodeo Drive a prostitute and sashayed back a princess. Many other women in Hollywood have made the exact same journey.

In a town where pilot shows don't get picked up because the lead is wearing the wrong shoes, how you dress is important. If you're a man, you should pull your teenage uniform of Converses and baseball hats out of the attic and wear them. Youth is worshipped in Hollywood, and as a result, many men have simply taken to wearing what an eight-year-old would. Or chinos.

If you're a female bluffer, you're going to need to get some work done (*see* Plastic Surgery, page 95), but clothes will help you some of the way. The best thing to do is buy a bunch of super-expensive shoes. If you can't afford these, buy a pair of black pumps from Primark and paint the soles Louboutin red. Job done.

A combination of the above applies if you are hoping to bluff your way as a Hollywood power lesbian.

MANICURE

This is not only a grooming issue, but also an opportunity for ostentatious displays of power. Hollywooders have been known to hire manicurists to work *under* boardroom tables while they're in meetings. Another trick is to hire a manicurist to work on your gnarled toes in your glass-fronted office (to the disgust of the minions in the bullpen outside). Some say it's a take on the traditional Maundy rite of the washing of the feet in Holy Week. Others say it's kind of gross and weird. Either way, nothing says 'serious about Hollywood' like a man wearing nail polish.

SUNGLASSES

These should be as silly as possible. For ladies, bigger and blingier is better. Gentlemen should consider buying the most extravagantly expensive ones they can afford. Both sexes should wear them all the time – and especially indoors.

THE TRADES

This refers to *Variety* and *The Hollywood Reporter*. Every morning, aspiring big shots drink their coffee and frown, perplexed, at these magazines. Here's the secret that none of them will tell you: no one understands *Variety* the first 200 times they read it. The magazine is specifically designed to confuse outsiders. It is written in its own language, with bizarre references to 'tyros' and 'tenpercenteries'. There is no need for a bluffer to grasp its contents (though there are helpful tips in the Glossary; *see* page 99). Having a copy ostentatiously close to your person is enough to let everyone know that you are a serious Hollywood player – even if you did buy it in WH Smith in Stevenage.

DEADLINE HOLLYWOOD

What everyone who's given up trying to understand *Variety* reads. It's a serious news website (*deadline.com*) in its own right, but it's also where insiders go to stitch each other up, under pseudonyms of varying opacity.

The site's noticeboards are excellent places to practice your bluffing skills by starting unfounded anonymous rumours about the denizens of Hollywood, at least until you get kicked off by the site's tenacious founder. Enjoy!

PEREZ HILTON

Perezhilton.com is one of Hollywood's most juicy and salacious websites. Mr Hilton is particularly known for drawing penises on photos of celebrities and giving them rather wonderful nicknames like Kiki Drunkst, Sluttylina and Cokate. He also had the dubious honour of prematurely announcing the death of Fidel Castro in 2007.

The lesson for the bluffer here is that you can't be right about everything all the time – and that Fidel Castro is a good deal more wily at the publicity game than your average starlet. Should he ever tire of his revolutionary activities, El Jefe Máximo could no doubt make millions as a publicist in Hollywood.

TMZ

Tmz.com is a website focusing on the indiscretions of the rich and famous. Since 2007 it has also been spun-off into a television show (the indiscretions of the rich and famous seemingly being too numerous for a website alone to address sufficiently). For gossip addicts, there is a TMZ bus tour that tootles around Los Angeles, giving tourists the opportunity to become real-life paparazzi as they document the lives of the glitterati of Beverly Hills.

The initials stand for 'Thirty-mile Zone', the area within Los Angeles that studios regard as 'local' for shooting purposes. Bluffers should affect a sour-faced distaste for all things gossipy – unless they, of course, are at the centre of it. As Oscar Wilde said: 'There is only one thing in life worse than being talked about, and that is *not* being talked about.'

PAPARAZZI

If you can't seem to get Perez Hilton or TMZ interested in your exploits then you may want to take extreme action. We're not talking about filming your own sex tape here, or setting up a fraudulent marriage that very publicly crashes and burns two days later. Those are old hat. Rather, we suggest you hire your own paparazzi to follow you around, even if the most exciting thing in your diary for the next two weeks is a trip to Tesco to pick up cat food.

We are not joking when we say that people actually do this in Hollywood. The first step is to post an advert on the internet for slightly annoying unemployed youngsters to start following you around with cameras. All you then need to do is go about your daily business, wearing slightly more revealing clothes than usual (extrovert female bluffers may take this a step further and attempt a few drunken fights in nightclubs, preferably wearing no knickers, etc., etc.). You will become a tabloid darling in no time.

AN IDEA

You don't really ever need to have one of these to succeed in Hollywood. Let other people do the hard work of thinking; you're bluffing. If ever put on the spot, talk enthusiastically about your idea for a film or television show being 'like *Downton Abbey* meets *Alien* meets *Top Gun* meets *Leaving Las Vegas*... but with Morgan Freeman'. If questioned further, sigh and mumble something along the lines of: 'Awfully sorry, but Harvey made me sign a strict NDA' (nondisclosure agreement).

A SCRIPT

Don't go to the trouble of writing one. Simply print a cover page with your name prominently displayed, then staple it to 110 pages of blank paper. Feel free to indulge in lengthy conversations about it with anyone you meet, particularly when you feel you have a captive audience (in a traffic jam, in a post office queue or on a lengthy airplane journey). Don't be disheartened by the fact that you have no actual material; movies have been greenlit without such pesky considerations as a script before.

A FRAMED PHOTO SIGNED BY A STAR/ PRODUCER/PRESIDENT

An eminent producer is known to leave signed and framed photographs of himself at every residence he visits, nestling them among the host's family portraits before he leaves. Though you are unlikely to be in his vicinity, you can adapt his MO to suit your own purposes, using chutzpah and Photoshop.

Carefully arranged photographs are a necessary signifier of success in Hollywood. They come in assorted categories and their positioning is important: place the signed headshot of a star on your bedside table (this denotes you have slept with them) and a framed photo of you with a US president anywhere (this denotes you shelled out upwards of $50,000 to attend a Hollywood fundraiser). A framed photo of yourself is also de rigueur for any space and an ideal gift for anyone. Don't be shy on this one: Hollywood is, after all, a town of endless self-promotion.

MOVIE POSTERS

One of these in French, Hungarian, German or Russian will proclaim you as a serious cinephile, even if you've never seen the original, let alone one in a foreign language. A poster in English, preferably with the box office take prominently displayed, will mark you out as someone who has made money in the movie world. Don't be concerned that the only relationship you had with the film was cutting the advert out of *Variety*. Advanced bluffers may consider signing it 'With thanks, [your name goes here], Johnny Depp.'

YIDDISH

You do not need to be Jewish in order to succeed in Hollywood. However, a few well-placed Yiddish words will go a long way to making it clear that you are skilled in the Hollywood vocabulary.

Not being Jewish is no bar to speaking Yiddish, and all denominations in Los Angeles use the language all the time. It has gone from being the limited property of a religion to a Hollywood shorthand. The following gems will come in handy (although we suggest self-restraint in the use of accent and gesticulation; we're not doing *Fiddler on the Roof* here).

Oy Vey 'Oh no!' Can be used to describe anything from a flat tyre to the box office takings of *John Carter.*

Bupkas Nothing. Can also be used to describe the box office takings of *John Carter.*

Chutzpah Nerve, balls, cojones.

Mazel tov 'Congratulations!' Rarely used, however, given that *Schadenfreude* is the more prevalent feeling in Hollywood.

Mishegoss Mischief, craziness: 'I would have made a billion dollars on *Batman*, if it weren't for that *mishegoss* with the nippled suit…'

Schmuck The end of a penis. Or a useless individual.

Shiksa Non-Jewish lady. These make another appearance in 'Trophy wives' (*see* page 90).

Advanced bluffers should also consider acquainting themselves with a working knowledge of the Jewish holiday calendar. Even if you're a Buddhist/Christian/ Moonie working in the local video store/B&Q/police

station, you should feel quite at home demanding the afternoon off for holidays such as Passover, Yom Kippur, Rosh Hashanah and Hanukkah.

The offices of Jewish and non-Jewish Hollywooders will be shut down at these times and you, a seasoned bluffer and enlightened human being, need to be *simpatico* with this. We also suggest you try your luck with the Hindu, Baha'i and Kwanzaa holidays – not necessarily because it's a Hollywood thing to do, but because, with all this bluffing, we believe you deserve as much rest as possible.

Marriages have formed and foundered on elaborate bluffs perpetrated by one actor against the other.

THE PLAYERS

There are various capacities in which you can bluff in Hollywood, and we encourage you to switch between them as necessary. Some will be harder to pull off than others. You may find it vexing, for instance, to convince people successfully that you starred in a film when they can simply watch it and see that you didn't (more ambitious bluffers should read the section on 'Plastic surgery', page 95, if they're not discouraged by this argument).

If you have had absolutely nothing to do with a film or television show, the safest thing to do is to claim that you produced it. Careers in Hollywood have been built on lesser bluffs. If you don't believe this, look at the arbitration process each year for the producer credits at the Oscars.

MOGULS

The Bluffers' Guide to Skiing defines moguls as 'big bumps in the snow'. In Hollywood we define them as anyone richer and more powerful than ourselves. Though, of course, as bluffers, we could never admit that.

AGENTS

Agents are the *über*-bluffers of the film and television industry. How else could they manage to persuade another person to give them 10% of everything they earn? Movie agents are the more dramatic operators, peeing out of windows, talking about raping and pillaging, imagining themselves as army commandants with loyal troops patrolling Wilshire Boulevard, etc., etc. – but the ace bluffers are the television agents.

Never try to out-bluff an agent.
Or date one.

Television agents are entitled to a packaging fee on any shows that their clients form a key part of. This fee allows them to take a percentage of the licence fee (what a network pays for the show) as well as the residuals. In some cases, the agents make more money on a television show than their clients. Through the policy of packaging, agents have perfected bluffing into a seven-figure art form. You have to admire them for it.

Never try to out-bluff an agent. Or date one.

ACTORS (AKA 'TALENT')

Although not as good at bluffing as agents, actors are in the same category through the virtue of being paid to lie. Great actors can bluff about anything, and often this seeps into their everyday lives, with the danger that sometimes they no longer know the difference between bluffing and real life. Marriages have formed and foundered on elaborate bluffs perpetrated by one actor against the other.

You should feel free to pontificate loudly on the number of actors who have married their co-stars: Vivien Leigh and Laurence Olivier (*Fire Over England*), Elizabeth Taylor and Richard Burton (*Cleopatra*), Angelina Jolie and Brad Pitt (*Mr and Mrs Smith*), Rachel Weisz and Daniel Craig (*Dream House*), LeAnn Rimes and Eddie Cibrian (**ahem*, Northern Lights*)...

STUDIOS

Studios are the cash cows of Hollywood. They are the Mr Moneybags of the whole shebang, the Johnny Big Potatoes of the party. This, you should tell your willing acolytes, is because they are the ones who generally stump up the cash for films and television shows.

Studios have a history of being owned by large corporations with more serious, grown-up interests than entertainment (mines, weapons, cable systems, funeral homes). This has made studios themselves expert bluffers, as they seek to justify how spending eight hours on a set with gorgeous movie stars qualifies as 'work' to a man who makes light bulbs for a living.

NETWORK PRESIDENTS

Network presidents are a small, elite group who spend a lot of time avoiding other people, as one of their main jobs is to say 'No'. Or to say 'No', then vociferously say: 'Yes, I told you so!' when it looks like a show is becoming a hit. They've been known to have their assistants check under their cars each time they leave parking lots.

They are often intellectuals who would have made excellent teachers, but instead have been co-opted by the consumer society into figuring out increasingly compulsive ways to get people to watch their channels – and adverts – and thus buy yet more rubbish they don't need. Network presidents are the nemeses of bluffers everywhere, because 90% of their job is listening, identifying and dealing with bulls**t.

EXECUTIVES

Executives are the gatekeepers of corporate money in Hollywood. As such, they are the preferred targets of the *über*-bluffers, the agents. Many executives fall by the wayside each year, turning their backs on the industry and instead plumping for the life of a microbrewery owner in Oregon. They have become exhausted by the idea of having to return another bullying phone call or to explain to yet another hopeful writer/director why his or her movie or television show is not being made. Others fall victim to internal politics about a character's wardrobe choices, the use of the subjunctive tense in a script, or the fact that they bought their boss a terrible Christmas present.

Executives assume that they are permanently on the verge of being fired. This is because they are. Any good executive can expect to be sacked at least twice in their career with the probability rising in proportion to their progress up the corporate ladder.

The good news is that the job description for an executive is rather woolly (although many would support 'harassed dogsbody' as a pithy summary), so you can claim to have 'been the executive on' the *Indiana Jones* franchise, *Desperate Housewives* or (closer to home) *Coronation Street* with relative impunity.

D-GIRLS

Not (in this case) an oblique reference to breast size. Here we are referring to 'development girls'. This is a derogatory term that can be applied to both men and women who are in the lower echelons of the business. Obviously, it's a lot more derogatory when applied to the male of the species.

MANAGERS

Managers are agents in sheep's clothing. While an agent may have dozens of clients, and can bluff each of them with enviable ease, managers focus their skills on a far smaller number. Managers often have a close relationship with their clients – so close in fact, that they convince the talent to allow them to 'produce' their movies and television shows.

This form of producing entails the manager showing up on the first day of shooting, demanding a private chef/ bigger trailer/yoga teacher for their client, then leaving before there's any danger of being involved in real work. You can state all this with absolute confidence, because it is true.

WRITERS

These dreamers come to Hollywood with the fantasy of being the next Billy Wilder and end up being the poor schmuck who writes *Killer Aliens Death Zone II.*

The majority of feature writers are sacked and replaced by other writers, who, in turn, are sacked. This pattern continues until many millions of dollars have been expended – all for the producers to return to the original script (*see* 'Development process', page 101).

Writers have more power in the television industry, where they can become show-runners and are then allowed to sack other writers.

However powerful, though, no writer is immune to the general Hollywood belief – and often stridently voiced opinion – that any director, producer, executive, actor or teamster on a project could do a better job of writing the script. These opinions are normally expressed in what is politely known as the 'notes call', after which most writers retreat to the comfort of their therapist's couch, the pub or a gun range.

DIRECTORS

A director is the captain of the ship. Unfortunately, Hollywood is traditionally a place where many other people think they're the captain, too. Not since the *Titanic*, in fact, has there been such an abundance of entitled, but frankly rather useless, upper-level nautical crew members.

As a director, you are responsible for pretty much everything on the set. Everything that goes wrong can be pinned on you. Many first-time directors have spoken about the fear they felt when first walking on a set.

Bluffers make very good directors, as they have to pretend that they are in charge of everything, all the time, when the truth is that they are frequently crying themselves to sleep in their trailers and making urgent calls to family, friends and agents to get them the hell out of there.

PRODUCERS

Good producers do everything – with the result that not many people know what they actually do. This makes them a great role model for a bluffer. Every year, many bluffers claim to have produced movies and television series that they had nothing to do with. The surprise on the faces of producers

Good producers do everything – with the result that not many people know what they actually do.

when they see clips of 'their' film at awards shows isn't grace or modesty. It's genuine confusion; many of these people have never clapped eyes on the movie before and have only the barest idea of what is going on around them.

There is an organisation in Hollywood known as the Producers Guild of America (PGA) that's trying to stop the proliferation of meaningless producer credits by introducing a 'Producers' Mark'. No one is quite sure what this is, but it's rumoured to entail branding 'PGA' on its various members' buttocks, like prize cattle.

Until there is an immediate danger of having to drop your trousers and expose your branded bottom, bluffers everywhere should feel safe talking about their 'producing' exploits.

INVESTORS

These are the nerdy monied types who hope to get substantial dividends (and a boost to their sex life) by investing in a Hollywood movie. They rarely get either. They are less imaginative and less risk-averse than bluffers and as such should be snubbed.

Unless, of course, you need cash for something.

ENTERTAINMENT LAWYERS

Lawyers are like agents, but with a degree behind them. As any bluffer will know, they are the brains behind the Hollywood operation. They are not as good at lying as agents (constrained by an ethical fealty to something called the 'law'), but they aren't to be trusted 100%, either. An agent will stab you in the back. A lawyer will stab you in the front. Then make you sign a waiver.

PR EXECUTIVES

PR executives (occasionally with the reassuring moniker 'Crisis' attached) are the lubricant that oils Hollywood's star-system machinery. They are useful for talking stars and starlets out of trouble/drunk-driving arrests/nicking stuff from Barneys. Every year a network tries to make a show about the PR industry. Every year they fail because no one can actually find their way through the lies to figure out what exactly these dark wizards of deception actually do.

As PR executives are simply bluffers by another name, you should be able to identify them at 500 yards. Nod politely, insinuating that you are aware you're in the presence of another master, and move on. There is no point talking to them because you can't believe a word they say.

CASTING DIRECTORS

Casting directors are frazzled individuals who seem to be always one audition away from a complete nervous breakdown. You should state this generalisation with a conviction that brooks further argument because it has the benefit of being mostly accurate. Casting directors can be pretty bad-tempered and often give the impression of being at the end of their rope in dealing with the idiocy around them (perhaps because they are having to deal with actors, directors, producers, and executives all day).

STAGE MOTHERS

You should never underestimate or insult a stage mother. They are the most ambitious and venomous of all the players in Hollywood. Adopt a tone of gravitas (or what passes for it) as you solemnly recount the time when a stage mother and an agent were locked in a room overnight with a pot of cash. In the morning, both were dead. And the money was gone.

EDITORS

Editors are excellent individuals but are rarely seen in daylight. They are locked in small rooms with a bunch of monitors and Cheetos corn puffs and given the task of spinning whatever dross a director has presented them with into movie gold.

Their circadian rhythm has replaced natural light with junk food, which gives them the ability to work for days on end without a break – just as long as the supply of trans fats and high-fructose corn syrup doesn't run dry.

COMPOSERS

Composers are another category of unsung heroes in Hollywood. Variety calls them 'cleffers'; those in the loop call them saints, due to their unflappable patience in listening to people with tin ears telling them how they want the theme song of a movie to sound ('De Dum Da Da De Dum… no, wait: Dum, Da, Da, DE DUM – hang on…').

After a couple of days of this, they normally put in their earplugs and write whatever they want. And who can blame them?

ASSISTANTS

Besides writers, these poor drudges are at the bottom of Hollywood's slippery totem pole. Stories abound of assistants being routinely humiliated, used as drug mules, or being made to pick all the red M&Ms out of candy jars. Sadly, most of these tales are true. Assistants are sustained by optimism, rich parents and an obsessional knowledge of *Jerry Maguire.*

Every bluffer should have an anecdote about the time they were an assistant. You shouldn't worry about making it unbelievably outlandish. Odds are that something quite like it probably genuinely happened to some poor b*****d.

SECOND ASSISTANTS

If you thought the life of an assistant was tough, try being the second assistant.

INTERNS

Honestly, for a similar quality of life, you would be better off joining the Foreign Legion.

WAITERS/BARTENDERS/PILATES TEACHERS

Also known as unemployed actors.

No one really drinks in LA or stays out past 8.30pm, so talking about the night you got completely plastered will mark you out as a rank amateur.

IT'S NOT WHAT YOU KNOW, IT'S WHO YOU KNOW

Bluffing about the Hollywood social scene is one of the most important skills you can acquire, whether you are in Bel Air (Los Angeles) or Bell End (Worcestershire). We don't expect you to actually *engage* with Angelenos (and in fact, we advise against it, as it can be the equivalent of trying to talk to a crocodile: quite treacherous and you're never really sure when you're going to lose a limb). There are, however, a few rules that will benefit anyone who wants to seem like they have friends in high places – or at least, Hollywood.

- When name-dropping, use only first names. Let your audience assume that when you mention 'Kate', 'Johnny' and 'Jack', it's Winslet, Depp and Nicholson, rather than Smith, Brown and Jones, your buddies from the local accountancy college.
- Make up zany hobbies you share with Hollywooders. The more outrageously healthy, the better. Never be afraid of crossing a line: there's nothing this bunch of nutjobs wouldn't do for vanity. A good start is

to combine two exercises into one word: Piloxing (Pilates and boxing), Yogalates (yoga and Pilates), Blufflates (bluffing and Pilates).

- No one really drinks in LA or stays out past 8.30pm, so talking about the night you got completely plastered will mark you out as a rank amateur. If you must, venture something along the lines of: 'Hey, I drank a whole litre of wheatgrass with Leonardo. It was, like, wild, man.'

- LA is a city that has some of the best restaurants in the world – and a population that has the pickiness of a seven-year-old when it comes to nutrition. Everyone here is allergic to something: gluten, shellfish, sugar, honesty. This is okay, because no one goes out to eat; they go out to be *seen*. Never talk about the quality of the meal you had in LA. Eating is for losers.

- Don't be shocked by any amount of back-stabbing, bitching and bullying; indeed, embrace descriptions of such behaviour in phoney accounts of Hollywood friendships. Any veteran will be able to list the times that he was shafted by his best friend/wife/parent/child/dog, and you should too. Relationships here are transactional and mostly fleeting. You need to be deft on your feet to survive. As a bluffer you will naturally have been endowed with almost superhuman charm, which will enable you to grin as you recount a story of Shakespearean betrayal, shrugging and telling your eager followers: 'That's just show business, kids.'

Combine these pointers with several touchstone spots you can reference glibly in conversation. The following are the places/activities you may safely claim to have formed the centre of your social life in Hollywood.

SOHO HOUSE

This private members' club has branches in London, Los Angeles, New York, Miami, Toronto and Berlin – you can choose any of them to bluff with as your favourite lunch spot with Angelina/Harrison/Johnny/Meryl/Leo.

The LA outpost is located on the top of an office block on Sunset, but is much nicer than that sounds. Say confidently: 'Knowing that all the little people are working away beneath you makes lunch so much more enjoyable.'

THE CHATEAU

Never call the Chateau by its full name: Chateau Marmont. This Hollywood institution has been around since 1927. It is a bluffer itself, pretending to be the Château d'Amboise in the Loire Valley, a castle after which it is modelled.

In 1498 King Charles VIII of France died at Château d'Amboise, and its pretender has also seen its share of celebrity deaths. John Belushi shuffled off his mortal coil after taking an overdose in one of the hotel's bungalows in 1982. Fashion photographer Helmut Newton passed away when he crashed his car into a wall on the property in 2004, and Jim Morrison used up 'the eighth of his nine lives' while ingeniously trying to access his hotel room from the window, rather than the door. (Rock stars will do anything to avoid lost-key charges.)

The best way to make an impact at the Chateau (or indeed, Hollywood) would seem to be to die in an outrageous manner there. As a bluffer, we suggest that

The best way to make an impact at the Chateau (or indeed, Hollywood) would seem to be to die in an outrageous manner there.

you don't go this far; it will be enough simply to mention drinking in the bar there with Kiki Drunkst. (For those with limitless ambition, *see* 'Hollywood Forever', page 53).

OPEN HOUSES

Hollywooders love nothing more than finding out how much each other is worth. Open houses offer excellent opportunities for this. Every weekend you will find *über*-agents, producers and starlets wandering around homes that are on the market. They have no intention of buying them; instead, they want to know what their neighbours' domains look like, and if they are better than theirs. It's the Hollywood equivalent of *Through the Keyhole*, but with the opportunity to open drawers and ask slightly pointed questions about square footage.

Touring the open houses of Billericay may not quite have the voyeuristic glamour of poking through people's belongings in Bel Air, but it does beat spending a Sunday afternoon watching the Grand Prix with your grandad. We recommend this as a great Hollywood tradition to adopt wherever you may be.

THE POLO LOUNGE

The Polo Lounge is where Old Hollywood goes to hobnob. It's located in The Beverly Hills Hotel, which is where Katharine Hepburn used to play tennis, apparently. It would be hard to bluff that you have seen her there (she went to the great multiplex in the sky in 2003), but you could probably get away with saying that you've sipped mojitos with Al Pacino by the pool, without raising too many eyebrows.

THE CHURCH OF SCIENTOLOGY, AKA CELEBRITY CENTRE INTERNATIONAL

This rather grand building is tucked away on Franklin Avenue in Hollywood. It is perhaps not the most traditional place to make friends. Unless, of course, you want them to be celebrities with a spiritual bent. This bluffer has never been inside the building, but she has spent many hours outside in an unmarked hatchback, pondering the mysterious events occurring inside, until the desperate need to answer a call of nature trumped her idle curiosity.

Scientology was founded as a religion in 1952 by L Ron

Hubbard, an American pulp fiction writer who believed in extraterrestrials. There has been much controversy surrounding the religion and, as bluffers living in a notoriously glass-like house, it is not for us to pass judgment. Or, more likely, we're just too scared of being sued.

Either way, Scientology is a useful tool for any bluffer because it is heavily associated with a Hollywood lifestyle through its celebrity adherents. You should recount, misty-eyed, the many rewarding evenings you spent being 'audited' (your soul, that is, not your taxes) and your adventures on the high seas as a member of something called the 'Sea Org'. Very few people will question your involvement, and anyone who tries to engage in further conversation should be quickly silenced by a furtive look around the room and a paranoid, whispered reference to 'walls having ears'.

HOLLYWOOD BOWL

The Hollywood Bowl is an outdoor concert hall carved into an Angeleno hillside. It has a capacity of almost 18,000 and so offers low-end rewards to social-climbing patrons who may be forced to mix with the hoi polloi. It is also one of the few places in LA where people are meant to be interested in something occurring outside of themselves (ever wondered why the theatre is so abysmally attended by Angelenos? It's because the lights go down and they can't be seen by anyone else in the audience).

Of course, the more inventive people still find a way of hogging the limelight despite the high-calibre acts there.

At the Bowl they sit closest to the front and eat, drink and network throughout the performances like latter-day Romans out for a night at the amphitheatre.

Bluffers should talk about the famous people they have met in the garden boxes at the Bowl, rather than the famous person they bought tickets to see on the stage. Great social climbing, like great sex, isn't about paying for it.

THE STAPLES CENTER

Floor seats at a Los Angeles Lakers game are the most sure-fire way of saying 'rich and famous' in Hollywood. For civilians, they will set you back upwards of $5,000 a ticket. That might seem ludicrously expensive, but it would allow you to rub shoulders with such luminaries as Jack (Nicholson), Dustin (Hoffman), Leonardo (DiCaprio), Jeffrey (Katzenberg) and mysterious Laker *über*-fan Yori, a female courtside fixture about whom very little is known.

Having only a limited knowledge of basketball should not intimidate the bluffer in this arena; all you need to know is that one overpaid tall guy beat another overpaid tall guy at putting a ball through a hoop. You should feel free to add personalised touches to tales of your time at the game to add colour and believability: buying Jack a Coke, eating Twizzlers with Jeffrey, etc., etc.

RUNYON CANYON

Runyon Canyon offers Angelenos another excellent way of multitasking. Rather than go to the pub with their mates,

Hollywooders arrange to climb a great big hill at six in the morning. It's not enough to be able to smile, nod and listen sympathetically to your buddy's problems; in Hollywood, you have to do this at altitude while performing a cardio-busting workout.

The upside is that you might see Gerard Butler or Scarlett Johansson overtake you as you struggle to catch your breath. In no circumstances do we advise that you actually attempt to build hiking into your repertoire – either in Hollywood or Hampstead. The physical toll it imposes on one's body is enough to drive even the most experienced bluffer to start telling nothing but the truth in exchange for a glass of water or an ambulance. Avoid this nonsense at all costs.*

YOGA

Yoga provides an excellent opportunity to pretend that you have met rich and famous people in Hollywood. Of course, we're not suggesting you actually have to take this up; as a bluffer, being able to talk convincingly about the time you did the downward dog with Nicole or Gwyneth is sufficient.

Hollywood yoga is rarely about chi and aligning one's chakras. Rather, it's about having a butt you could bounce a ten-pence piece off. So don't adopt the zen attitude of a guru: yoga here is about passive-aggressive mat placement and hernia-inducing designer gym wear.

*If you can't, then be sure to get a copy of *The Bluffer's Guide to Hiking.*

GETTING AWAY FROM IT ALL

Hollywooders, like regular people, do occasionally feel the strain and need to get away from it all. For times when yoga and chanting – and even, godammit, that much-regretted helping of carbs after dusk – is not enough to drive away the box-office blues, a trip out of town is necessary. Unfortunately, there are few places that are judged capable of standing up to the extreme demands of Hollywood folk, and, more often than not, they will see the very person they were hoping to avoid on their getaway sitting poolside across from them. We have included a list of favourite bolt-holes, so read on.

ASPEN

Aspen is the winter residence of many Hollywood celebs. The skiing is meant to be great – though that is unimportant to any bluffer, as your time there will have been spent strictly talking business with the moguls during après-ski while wearing enough fur to empty a small zoo.

MALIBU

This '27 miles of scenic beauty' along the Pacific Coast Highway is a great place for any bluffer to reference. Many Hollywooders who have already made their pile have their main residences in Malibu: the terrible traffic and threats of landslide, wildfire and tsunami don't seem to impinge on the optimistic lifestyles of people who have millions in the bank.

Celebrity-spotting here is rare, however, as the big

shots tend to stay behind closed doors or on their private beaches. More modest bluffers (but where's the fun in that?) may eschew a mention of having spent the weekend at Charlize's beachside property for a casual spotting of Nick (Nolte) at the Malibu Country Mart. We leave it to your discretion.

OJAI

Ojai (pronounced *Oh Hi*) is a tiny place 80 miles north of Los Angeles in Ventura County. The town is rumoured to be on a 'power spot', but more reliable wattage is always found at the Ojai Valley Inn, which is the hotel of choice for moguls looking to get away from it all – or to get married. Tell friends that, like many Hollywooders, your first marriage took place at the Inn. And that your second one will take place in your pre-nup lawyer's office, as you protect your remaining assets by forcing your new spouse to sign the agreement in blood.

SITE OF ANY NATURAL DISASTER

We know this is cynical, and we're not for one moment suggesting that you follow natural disasters around the world in order to rub shoulders with the Hollywood elite and gain publicity. That would be despicable.

But if there *happened* to be a calamity not *too* far away that you could go to with, say, a couple of dozen paparazzi and a few bottles of mineral water and first-aid kits... well, then, it may not be such a bad thing.

If you know what we're saying.

Not that we're saying anything.

Particularly not about the power of celebrity to exploit tragedy for its own ends.

No, siree.

VEGAS

As a bluffer there are a few guidelines to be aware of when you begin to regale your admiring followers with the account of your marvellous trip to Sin City with the bigwigs. Just remember:

- You took the jet there; you most certainly did *not* fly commercial.
- Your room was comped by Steve Wynn himself.
- Celine dedicated a song to you in her set.
- Everything was perfect until Russell lost his card in a strip club and punched a bouncer.

GETTING FURTHER AWAY FROM IT ALL: HOLLYWOOD FOREVER

It may be reassuring for bluffers to know that even in death there is a strict social system in Hollywood. This can be seen most clearly at Hollywood Forever, the cemetery of the stars. It was founded in 1899, and anyone who was anyone is resting here: Harry Cohn, Cecil B DeMille, Florence Lawrence, Jayne Mansfield, Rudolph Valentino and Douglas Fairbanks (Jnr and Snr) are among the celebrity inhabitants.

The fact that entry is predicated on the virtue of being dead may confound the bluffer... if only temporarily.

Nonetheless there is arguably some advantage to be gained by letting it be known that you find solace in sitting by your 'mentor's' grave, perusing the scripts from his/her most famous movies. Very few people will swallow this sort of preposterous nonsense, but you never know.

This is Hollywood, after all.

FILM-SET JARGON

There is only so much a book can teach you about the interactions on a set. One solution would be to steer well clear of a situation in which you found yourself on a set, lest you start tripping over dollies and gaffers and all the other necessary contraptions and personnel needed in modern-day filmmaking.

Let's be frank: film sets are dirty, disorganised and often boring places (you should note that because of runaway production costs many of them are now in Canada). Stay away from them whenever you can. Many moguls have achieved great power and success without ever having to sully their Gucci loafers by traipsing about on a set.

In fact, this may be *why* they have achieved great power and success.

If you do find yourself in the unfortunate position of having to be in the middle of the action, we recommend that you find a quiet place and settle in with this book, re-emerging to shout about 'checking the gate', 'clearing the eyeline' and 'flipping the lens', and then triumphantly stalking off to the safety of craft services, which you will need to know is the unit providing the food and beverages on set (*see* page 59).

You must have more than a passing familiarity with the following lingo, so commit as much of it to memory as a bluffer's limited attention span permits.

Above the line This is most commonly what most bluffers are, as 'above the line' personnel tend to have rather muddy qualifications. It normally refers to the star, director, producer or writer. Everyone else (i.e., 'below the line') actually has a job description and a measure of accountability.

Action! Normally only the director says this. Some directors seek greater motivation for their team by firing a gun in lieu of shouting (Samuel Fuller, for instance, reportedly carried a Luger to set). Under no circumstances will bluffers ever utter the word 'action'. This is mainly because they never have any intention of taking any.

AD Assistant director. As a bluffer would never admit to being an assistant anything, you should ignore this moniker, though not the person holding it, as he/she is often the only thing standing between a director and his/her nervous breakdown.

Best boy The best boy is officially the second in command in an electrical department. As in any industry, this means that he (or she these days) tends to get stuck with the grunt work. At least in Hollywood they get a nice title.

BG Background. Something into which the bluffer should never fade.

Blow job No, not a hangover from the esteemed *Bluffer's Guide to Sex*. Rather, this is when you clean a camera lens with a can of compressed air.

Buff and puff No, still not a reference to *The Bluffer's Guide to Sex*. This is when an actor is sent to hair and make-up.

Call sheet This gives the times when everyone should be on set. It is ranked by importance, with the lead actor being 'number one'. Of course, as a bluffer, you can ignore this, safe in the knowledge that you are the most important person on the set.

C47 A fancy Hollywood name for a clothes peg. This is more likely to be seen in the kit of someone 'below the line', so may not be an appropriate piece of equipment for a bluffer to sport, given your aversion to real, actual work. It's used for clipping stuff to other stuff. That is all you need to know.

Check the gate This is the last thing you do before moving the set-up. The film gate is the opening in the front of a movie camera. Scenes have been known to be ruined after a whole morning of shooting when a hair or scratch has been found 'in the gate'. This is an amateur mistake that no bluffer would make, particularly if you stay safely away from the camera and any kind of responsibility. Usually the AD calls out 'Check the gate!' when the crew is about to move on to the next shot. This gives him/her something to do.

Chewing the scenery (Antonym: mailing it in; *see* page 62). Any time an actor *really* goes for it – especially if he or she is not meant to. It is the thespian equivalent of playing Hamlet when you are meant to be Rosencrantz or Guildenstern.

Clapper loader The fancy name for the clapper loader is the second assistant camera. This guy or gal loads the film stock into camera magazines and operates the clapperboard: the wooden or plastic board that is held in front of the camera and snapped together at the start of filming each scene. A clapperboard (aka slate, slate board, sync slate, time slate, sticks, board, marker, etc.) is an excellent item for any bluffer to acquire and display prominently. You can buy non-electronic ones from Amazon for about £10, and personalise them to hint at your fictitious involvement in the movies.

'Clear the lens' is Hollywood talk for 'Get the f*** out of the way!'

Clear the lens This is Hollywood talk for 'Get the f*** out of the way!' This phrase is usually uttered by irate camera operators who are trying to line up a shot. You shouldn't take this personally, as they often yell the converse: 'Find the lens!' to encourage actors to figure out where the camera is. Which, as an actor, would seem to be one of your main jobs. Cameras also tend to be rather large, which should make the task of identifying one easy.

Clear the eyeline The actor's retort of choice. These poor devils may have been yelled at to find the camera, to take their clothes off, to walk and talk in a certain way, to kiss an ugly co-star with a fondness for chewing garlic before scenes… this phrase is the silver bullet in their defensive arsenal.

Actors can explain poor performances by claiming to be distracted by a crew member, director, cloud or alien that is in their eyeline. Several years ago an actor well-known for playing Batman went apoplectic on a film set because some minion was in his eyeline. He demanded the prompt sacking of this poor lackey. What Batman failed to realise (his superhuman powers letting him down in this unfortunate moment) was that there are many cameras on a film stage. His outburst was recorded and posted online, forcing our shamefaced superhero to make a very public apology.

Craft services A great place for a bluffer to hang out while attempting to avoid responsibility of any kind. Craft services is basically a mobile cafeteria. For bluffers who will never venture west of Cardiff, you might consider designating your kitchen as 'craft services' and telling any guests that you are 'popping to crafty' when you offer to make them a cuppa. If you can arrange for a kindly middle-aged lady to be on hand there (who is not recognisably your mum), so much the better.

Day out of days This biblical-sounding phrase describes the chart that tells everyone when actors are needed for shooting. With your chronic fear of film sets you should aim to be on this as little as possible. It is always more productive to bluff in absentia.

Dailies These are DVDs or internet links of the filming that took place the day before. They are sent to poor, nameless executives who are forced to watch 500 shots of something prosaic to make sure that their studio's money is being well spent. They may then call the producer or director (or anyone else who will take their calls) to make oblique and annoying comments on the dailies as a way of exacting revenge for the grind their life has become. The best comments focus on aspects of shooting that can no longer be changed or have nothing to do with the dailies, such as music notes.

Doris Day parking The best parking space on the lot. It is, of course, de rigueur for all bluffers, in all places and at all times. In the unlikely instance that such a spot has not been provided, make your own placard with your name proudly displayed and plant it in the ground to stamp your territory, like a latter-day imperial colonist. This trick is as effective on a lot in Hollywood as in a car park at your local Waitrose.

DP Aka director of photography. DPs are in charge of how everything on the screen looks. They are responsible for the lighting, setting up the shot and the camera moves. Give anyone 'director' as part of their title and there is a great likelihood that pretty soon they will start to act a little above themselves. As such, seasoned DPs can often be enough to send first-time directors running for the hills.

Four-banger A trailer with four dressing rooms. In Hollywood, the size of your trailer is indicative of your status on set. Bluffers should beware of talking loudly about their 12-banger. It's yet to be invented.

French hours This is a day on set when no time for lunch is allotted. It is a rare example of American irony because, as everybody knows, lunch in France is not only obligatory, but a rather lengthy affair.

Gaffer The head electrician. Can be used for anyone who is heading anything. We would suggest you adopt this as part of your on-set persona, although the thought that you may have to start tinkering with the electrics is somewhat alarming.

Grips Anyone who moves anything on a set. Grips can be quite feisty about this, which is a good thing for bluffers as it provides you with more of an excuse to sit on your butt as other people work around you.

Honeywagon Warning: this is not as pleasant as it sounds. Do not be fooled. Honeywagons are the crew's washrooms.

In the can No, we are not referring to the honeywagon. This is when a scene has been shot and completely finished.

Lewinskys Kneepads that are used by stuntmen. You can probably figure out where the name comes from.

Lock-off A camera that has been secured and is ready for action. The very worst thing a bluffer could do is blunder into it. Again, best avoided by being nowhere near a set.

Mailing it in (Antonym: chewing the scenery; *see* page 57.) In many professions, 'mailing it in' is a perfectly admirable way of climbing the career ladder. If you do provide substandard work, there are very few occasions when you are caught doing so: the corporate world is full of second chances, excuses, endless performance reviews and obfuscations.

The same is not true of the acting world. If your acting doesn't manifest the particular enthusiasm required, it is rather obvious pretty quickly – which is why acting is only to be recommended as an occupation for the advanced bluffer.

Martini The last shot of the day. And by that time, you might very well need one.

Pan Not something you fry your eggs in. This is when a camera swings horizontally to cover a scene. Fearless bluffers should refer to the pan shot, panning and scanning and (for the truly brave) the pan-tilt-zoom camera.

Production assistant (PA) Aka dogsbody.

Pick-up When a scene simply cannot be shot from beginning to end as it is written, the director may elect to do a 'pick-up'. This involves starting in the middle of things and ignoring the problems that have gone before, with the aim of cutting together a better version in the editing room. If only we could do that in real life…

Second unit This is where the action isn't. Second units shoot the bits that directors do not want to. This is because they often do not include the principal talent, are complicated (stunts and special effects) or simply dangerous.

Sound stage This is a large soundproof warehouse-type building found on studio backlots. There are a few famous sound stages that you may want to slip into conversation. The 007 stage is located at Pinewood Studios in England.

Acting is only to be recommended as an occupation for the advanced bluffer.

It was originally built in 1976 to film *The Spy Who Loved Me*. Unfortunately, it has burned down twice since then, but rebuilding has ensured that it is now the second-largest stage in Europe.

The largest sound stage in the US is Stage 15 at Sony in Culver City, California. It was the original sound stage for *The Wizard of Oz*; more recent productions include *Men in Black* and *Spiderman*.

Many US studios avoid using the numbers seven and 13 when naming sound stages for superstitious reasons. Normally we would scoff at this, but the unfortunate history of the 007 stage would seem to counsel caution.

Steadicam When a human turns into a camera. Bluffers should always refer to Steadicam shots as having been responsible for some of the most remarkable sequences in film, such as the chase scenes in *Marathon Man*. Don't worry if you haven't seen the film: this shouldn't stop you from expounding on its technical merits at length.

Tech scout The tech scout happens when the director tours a location with all the department heads (camera, sound, electrical, grip, etc.). The idea is to spot problems before they occur in a shoot. Sometimes that doesn't happen and disaster ensues. As such, the tech scout is something for any bluffer to steer well clear of so that he or she can maintain plausible deniability (the gold standard of bluffing).

Turnaround One of Hollywood's rather more splendid aspects is that it makes contracts for how much time you *don't* have to spend at work. Turnaround is the time off that is guaranteed to actors and crew members between shooting days.

There is another form of turnaround in Hollywood: when a studio gives a project back to its creators because it is no longer planning to make it. This is much more disappointing. We advise bluffers to focus on the former of these two definitions given that forced unemployment is better by far than actual unemployment.

Video village If your excuses about dead hamsters, gammy legs and ergophobia (the bluffer's friend: fear of work) have not cut the mustard and you actually have to be on a set, this is the safest place to hang out. The video village is centred around a couple of monitors that show the action that is being shot. Many directors can get very territorial about who can sit in and be near the video village. Martin Scorsese is rumoured to erect a mirror on the top of the monitors in his village to watch for encroachers.

As a bluffer, such concerns are beneath you as your mindset rightly cannot countenance anything but a warm welcome wherever you may choose to roam. You should confidently approach the village, grab a chair (ideally not one with someone else's name on it), put on a pair of headphones and smile encouragingly at the other villagers. Every now and then clap loudly and shout 'Whoa, Nelly! That's a good one!' regardless of the action taking place in front of you.

Motivated bluffers may elect to start their own film festivals. These can be held in your living room and consist of watching black-and-white movies non-stop for three days while wearing the same pants.

FILM FESTIVALS

Film festivals are held every few months and offer the bluffer an excellent excuse for random disappearances, or the semblance of them. While you may have spent January in your sickbed with something unfashionable like gout, other people might reasonably assume that you were at Sundance in Park City, Utah. Canny bluffers will be able to structure their years around the dates of film festivals and thus avoid having to participate in any of their more tedious daily duties, such as profitable employment, family time or engaging in serious relationships.

More motivated bluffers may even elect to start their own film festivals. These can be held in your living room and consist of watching black-and-white movies non-stop for three days while wearing the same pants. The important thing about any film festival is that 1) you talk about it loudly as a way of professing your (vastly exaggerated) knowledge of the medium, and 2) you invent bizarre mascots that will also function as trophies (golden bears, flying lions, palm leaves).

HISTORY

There is some debate about who holds the honour of hosting the first film festival. This is because they originated in Europe; as anyone who has attempted to get on a ski lift in a European resort will know, consensus about who was first in line is almost impossible to achieve. Venice seems to hold the record as the first internationally recognised film festival, starting in 1932. However, British bluffers would be within their rights to point out that, in 1925, the London Film Society (whose founding members included HG Wells and George Bernard Shaw) started screenings of films that were banned in many European cinemas. It may not be the first example of a film festival, but it was certainly the first example of a British fascination with films from the Continent that weren't primarily pornographic in focus.

Once Venice jumped in, other European nations got involved. Joseph Stalin, for instance, was a massive movie buff. He not only had screening rooms in all his palaces but, like the development executive from hell, would 'offer' filmmakers master classes in their art. You should adopt a tone of great solemnity when you pronounce that the Dear Father's favourite film was *Tarzan the Ape Man.* As a result of such enthusiasm, the Moscow Film Festival was founded in 1935.

The French were next, founding the Cannes Film Festival in 1939. In typical Gallic fashion, it lasted one glorious night, then wasn't seen again for seven years.

The post-war years saw a blossoming of film festivals.

Point out pedantically that the Edinburgh International Film Festival started in 1947 and holds the honour of being the longest continuous film festival in the world. Berlin's Berlinale began in 1951. By 1957, the USA had adopted the idea, too, with the San Francisco International Film Festival. It wasn't until 1978 that the Sundance Film Festival was born, in its first guise as the Utah/US Film Festival.

FILM FESTIVALS TODAY

At some stage you may need to explain to your boss/ spouse/children what you were (allegedly) doing at a festival, and so a rudimentary idea of what happens at them is desirable. Many people go because they have made a film and want to sell it. Others go because they want to find new talent to represent. And a third catch-all category comprises those who are hangers-on and have access to ridiculously generous expense accounts and harbour no shame about using them.

There are also people who go because they simply like watching films. We caution bluffers to avoid such enthusiasts, as they are likely to have a genuine curiosity about what is going on.

SUNDANCE FILM FESTIVAL (JANUARY)

Sundance, in Utah, is where all the Hollywood execs go to escape their families after the gruelling Christmas period. The fact that the mountain resort is also a fashionable skiing destination plays absolutely no part in their decision to relocate there for a week or so. Though you may never have been, nor are ever likely to go, you should assume a distant look of piety when talking about the 'commercialisation' of Sundance, and how the vibe has changed since *Sex, Lies, and Videotape* first debuted there in 1989. This is nonsense, of course; every year fascinating new films are found at Sundance, but you need not handicap yourself with these facts, as a stridently voiced opinion is more important than a well-researched argument.

If by any chance you should find yourself in Sundance in January, the best thing you can do is outfit yourself *à la* James Bond circa *The Spy Who Loved Me.* You may not be able to get into any of the screenings (buying tickets can be notoriously tricky), but at least you can impress the

No one need ever know that the closest you got to Utah was watching a reality show about polygamist sister wives.

locals with your banana-yellow ski suit and derring-do on the slopes. Don't forget to say that you're a regular ski buddy of 'Bob's'. This is a reference to Robert Redford who put Sundance Resort on the map when he acquired it in 1969 (and named it after his character in *Butch Cassidy and the Sundance Kid*).

Maximum bluffing points are earned for knowing

that the resort's original name was the rather less inviting 'Timp Haven', and that the film festival is held primarily in Park City – a much bigger mountain resort approximately 30 miles north. Even more bluffing points are on offer for knowing that Bob got seriously into skiing after playing the cocksure David Chappellet in *Downhill Racer*.

When you 'return home' (assuming you ever left), you should speak about snowboarding with Woody (Harrelson), hanging out with Michael (Moore) at the lodge and discussing film noir with the Coen brothers at the Eccles.

No one need ever know that the closest you got to Utah was watching a reality show about polygamist sister wives.

THE BERLINALE: BERLIN INTERNATIONAL FILM FESTIVAL (FEBRUARY)

The Germans say that the Berlinale is where the deals get done. Yet the Germans have claimed many outrageous things before (mostly about items belonging to them that patently do not, such as sun loungers and smaller countries) and we suggest that you approach their feisty bravado with weary resignation.

Expert bluffers may wish to express a conviction that the Berlinale is the most political of all the film festivals, and point to a time in 1970 when the whole jury resigned after failing to reach a consensus on Michael Verhoeven's film *O.K.*

In 1979 the Soviet delegation walked out after the

inclusion of *The Deerhunter.* Such controversies can be a useful tool for the bluffer. Should anyone catch you at home in your pyjamas when you were meant to be at the Kino in Berlin, you should tell them that you were so outraged by the portrayal of the well-to-do chuffies of Notting Hill/Kensington/Hammersmith in a movie you saw there that you simply had to leave. It might be one thing for the Europeans to play fast and loose with the history of the Vietnamese, but when it comes to the misrepresentation of affluent West Londoners, you simply could not condone it.

FESTIVAL DE CANNES (MAY)

Cannes is often regarded as the most glamorous of the top-tier film festivals. Celebrities arrive for the red carpet in their tuxedos, but real stars make do with a pair of skimpy Speedos and a jaunt along the beachfront. The trend for being photographed on the beach in Cannes was arguably started by Jean-Paul Sartre in 1947 (although he chose the philosopher's uniform of choice: a rather stuffy-looking white woolly polo neck). Brigitte Bardot realised the publicity power of a good photo in her bikini and revolutionised Sartre's look by showing up in a small two-piece. Not one to be outdone by the ladies, Arnold Schwarzenegger appeared in a much tinier outfit a couple of decades later. Bluffers may like to refer here to a look that satirist Clive James famously described as similar to 'a condom full of walnuts'. The 'Arnie' cannot be advocated for bluffers, as it removes a key requisite:

room for the imagination of one's audience.

Such a louche attitude to propriety means that it is generally pretty hard to upset anyone at Cannes, although Lars von Trier managed it in 2011 after making some rather unfortunate comments about Hitler.

VENICE INTERNATIONAL FILM FESTIVAL (SEPTEMBER)

Venice hosts one of the oldest film festivals in the world, and like the Moscow Film Festival, it once received the support of its country's dictator. Benito Mussolini was not just a fan of the movies, but also movie stars, and reportedly sent American actress Anita Page up to eight letters a week. These were addressed to her simply as: 'Film star Anita Page, MGM Hollywood', and in addition to proposals of marriage and mentions of her bosom, often included signed photographs of himself, which he fervently hoped to trade for one of her.

Sadly, Il Duce's passion was never consummated. His influence on the festival also waned, and in 1942 the practice of handing out the Mussolini Cup to festival winners was stopped.

The Venice International Film Festival may have many prestigious claims to fame, but surely the best one is that they ship the celebrities there by boat. Few things are more charming than seeing a starlet attempting to disembark from a boat while perched on five-inch heels.

Stars may not flounce around half-dressed here as in Cannes, but you may see a quasi-celebrity bravely enduring a run along the Lido. Bluffers will not engage in this kind of naked attention-grabbing; they will be too busy ensconced in one of the bars at the Cipriani.

TORONTO INTERNATIONAL FILM FESTIVAL (TIFF) (SEPTEMBER)

Those plucky Canadians decided that they could compete with the glamorous festivals of Europe and established a film gathering in fashionable Toronto. Toronto may not have the beachfront of Cannes, the Lido of Venice or the history of Berlin, but it is 90 minutes away from half of Niagara Falls. Given that many filmmakers view their craft as akin to putting oneself in a wooden barrel and plunging into a dangerous abyss, Toronto was seen as the ideal place to celebrate the movies.

Many people say that the TIFF is a good indicator of Oscar picks. Then again, they also say this about the Directors Guild of America Awards, the Producers Guild of America Awards, the BAFTAs and the Golden Globes. The best indicator of success at the Oscars is actual success at the Oscars.

Being Canadian, Toronto doesn't have the impudence of the French, the efficiency of the Germans or the competitiveness of the Americans. If questioned about the Toronto festival, the best description for bluffers to use is simply 'nice'.

DEAUVILLE, EDINBURGH, LOS ANGELES, DUBAI, SOUTH BY SOUTHWEST (SXSW), TELLURIDE, TRIBECA, LONDON

These are all respectable film festivals and are certainly worth a bluff if you need a long weekend away from your family.

Bluffers needn't bother getting buffed, puffed and drunk at the Governor's Ball. Tell colleagues you'll be there, then lock yourself in your flat for the weekend and watch the event on television in your pyjamas.

KUDOS

Like a benevolent but manic headmaster, Hollywood seems to dish out awards for almost everything. There are prizes for acting, writing, directing, clothes, hair, make-up... there are even awards for foreigners. Any small measure of success can be lauded in Hollywood.

A necessary part of convincing others that you are a Hollywood player is an acquaintance with the many gongs of the industry – even if you stand as much chance of receiving one as being struck by lightning (a respectable one in a million in your lifetime). There are several important ceremonies about which you need to impress an audience with your insider knowledge.

THE OSCARS

The first Academy Awards ceremony was held in May 1929 at the Hollywood Roosevelt Hotel. It was actually held three months after the winners had been announced. While this may not have demonstrated the most astute showmanship, it did relieve the 270 members of the audience from the tedium of having to listen as winners, pretending to be shocked, stood at the podium blubbing like four-year-olds as they accepted their awards.

There is some dispute about where the name 'Oscar' originated. This is not surprising, given Hollywood's penchant for taking credit where it isn't due. Some claim that Bette Davis named the statuette after her first husband, bandleader Harmon Oscar Nelson; others say that an employee of the Academy of Motion Picture Arts and Sciences (AMPAS, or 'the Academy') commented that it looked like her Uncle Oscar and the name stuck. A third school of thought contends that Louis B Mayer's secretary mentioned that it looked like the Scandinavian king Oscar II – though how she had seen him naked remains unclear.

What is indisputable, however, is the identity of the model for the Oscar statuette. This was Emilio 'El Indio' Fernández. El Indio, a prison escapee from Mexico, was rumoured to be in love with Dolores del Río, the wife of MGM art director Cedric Gibbons. Dolores never returned his affection, but did convince El Indio to pose naked for her husband as he crafted the Oscar design. One can only imagine what this did for El Indio's pride, as he stood naked on a podium while his sweetheart's husband chiselled a replica of his manhood. His self-respect received further blows when he later became an esteemed writer, director and actor, yet never managed to receive the golden trophy for his own creative endeavours.

Getting hold of an Oscar without having to do any work is pretty hard, not least because the Academy has been clamping down on its credit system in recent years.

But don't let this deter you. There are a couple of options audacious bluffers can consider. The first is to double-bluff by declining an Oscar (even, and especially, if you haven't been awarded one). You may have impressed your friends and colleagues with the idea that you are a Hollywood big shot, but the lack of awards on your mantelpiece tells a different story. To combat this, tell your acolytes that you were awarded a gong, but decided to turn it down.

Getting hold of an Oscar without having to do any work is pretty hard... But don't let this deter you.

Writer Dudley Nichols was the first brave soul to do this in 1936, citing a dispute between the Writers Guild of America and the Academy. Actor George C Scott declined an Oscar for his role in *Patton*, telling the Academy that the ceremony was 'a two-hour meat parade' and 'demeaning' (although many actors would describe both of these humiliations as a typical day at the office). Marlon Brando also refused his award for *The Godfather* in protest at Hollywood's treatment of Native Americans. He sent Sacheen Littlefeather in his place to read a 15-page diatribe listing his concerns. This moment is also in the history books as having been one of the few instances of an actor voluntarily giving someone else his lines.

The second option for bluffers is perhaps more straightforward. It also has the benefit of being as patriotic and American as apple pie and the Fourth of July. It is, of course, cold hard cash. While the winners (and heirs) of all Oscars awarded after 1950 have to sign an agreement giving the Academy first dibs on buying back an Oscar, no such rules apply to winners pre-1950. The good news for bluffers is that all you need is a piddling $1.5 million dollars and a statuette can be yours.

Buying such kudos would land you in interesting company: Michael Jackson purchased the Oscar for *Gone with the Wind* in 1999 and magician David Copperfield is reported to keep the Best Director Oscar for *Casablanca* in his bedroom.

THE EMMYS

The Emmys are to television what the Oscars are to film. The first meeting of the Television Academy, as it was originally known, took place in 1946. At the time, only 4,000 homes in Los Angeles had television sets, so it may have come as little surprise to founder Syd Cassyd that only five people showed up for the first gathering. However, Cassyd, who served under Frank Capra in the Second World War, was not one to be put off easily. A week later, perhaps with the promise of better snacks, free alcohol and taxis home, the numbers had increased fivefold to an heroic 25. By the fifth meeting, Cassyd had a respectable audience figure of 250.

The story behind the design of the Emmy has no such

benighted romantic hero as the Oscar's El Indio. As television is often seen as the more sensible, less showy cousin of film, so, too, is the history of its statuette less dramatic. It goes like this: television engineer Louis McManus used his wife as the model, depicting her with wings, holding an atom. The wings are meant to represent the muse of art; the atom is the electron of science.

Because television production is often driven by committee, with everyone who is (not even) anyone having a viewpoint, it may not surprise bluffers to learn that the Television Academy turned down 47 other designs before adopting McManus's. Ferocious arguments about the statuette's hair, make-up, weight, wardrobe and the possibility of enhancing her looks with Botox no doubt took place before the final decision was made. As to the name, 'Immy' was its original form, taken from the term for a particular type of television camera. This was later changed to 'Emmy' as being better suited to the female statue.

When the first, modest Emmy ceremony took place in 1949, AMPAS members were voting that year for adaptations of famous literary works (*Mildred Pierce, The Picture of Dorian Gray*) and films dealing with social issues such as alcoholism (*The Lost Weekend*). Emmy members were determined to keep it all light, bright and cheery in the television world. As such, the first winner of an Emmy was the little-known Shirley Dinsdale. Shirley was a 20-year-old ventriloquist from UCLA, the lead of children's show *Judy Splinters*. Other winners that year included *Pantomime Quiz* for 'Most Popular Program'.

It is shocking that people dare to say that television is responsible for the dumbing down of popular culture.

The Academy of Television Arts & Sciences is now a well-established organisation and awards body. Each year hundreds of television stars and execs dust off their tuxedos and head to downtown LA to celebrate their achievements (or at least, in the brutal world of television, the fact that they have survived another season).

Bluffers needn't bother getting buffed, puffed and drunk at the Governors Ball. Tell colleagues you'll be there, then lock yourself in your flat for the weekend and watch the event on television in your pyjamas. Get a spray tan and return to the office on Monday, talking loudly about how funny Jimmy Fallon was and how they shut the bar in the Nokia Theatre auditorium during the intervals. This is pretty much all that the network and studio execs will be able to remember about the evening anyway.

THE GOLDEN GLOBE AWARDS

This is the boozy, fun sister of Hollywood award shows. It is run by the Hollywood Foreign Press Association, the 'Foreign' part of which may explain the emphasis on misbehaviour that comes with the awards. The Globes cover both film and television.

One of the best parts of the Golden Globes is the tradition they have for electing a 'Miss Golden Globe' annually. Each January, some poor young lady is asked to serve in this capacity, which requires buying a pretty frock and ignoring the rather overt reference in the title to 'gazungas'. More often than not, she suffers the double misfortune of being the offspring of a celebrity (although the advantage of this is that she will already be used to dealing with embarrassing public behaviour). Veterans of this honour include Melanie (Griffith), Laura (Dern), Joely (Fisher) and Rumer (Willis). Occasionally, Miss Golden Globe is actually a man – as was the case with Freddie (Prinz, Jr), in 1996. At least he didn't have to wear a dress.

THE BAFTA AWARDS

Though not a Hollywood tradition strictly speaking, the British Academy of Film and Television Arts (BAFTA) Awards are a pretty important fixture on the awards calendar – at least for British people. BAFTA is one of the many ways Brits try to keep their end up in Hollywood. Others include:

- A stubborn refusal to lose their accent, as they believe it makes them sound more clever than Americans.
- A generally phoney claim to know the royal family – or at least Pippa Middleton.
- An unswerving (literally) loyalty to driving on the wrong side of the road.

The BAFTAs are all very admirable and it's fun to see the Brits rather cack-handedly trying to straighten and bleach their teeth, body hair and skin to fit in with their more polished American counterparts. The best and worst thing you can say about a BAFTA is that it isn't an Oscar.

THE GOLDEN RASPBERRY AWARDS (AKA 'THE RAZZIES')

The Golden Raspberries were founded to reward the very worst achievements in film each year. They give Hollywood the rare opportunity to laugh at itself.

The Razzies were founded in 1981 by publicist and copywriter John JB Wilson. Categories include 'Worst Actor', 'Worst Actress', 'Worst Screen Couple' (this is often a reference to breasts), 'Worst Screenplay', 'Worst Prequel/ Remake/Rip-Off/Sequel'.

Occasionally there are years when special categories are deemed necessary to cover the many offences committed by Hollywood: 'Worst Screenplay Grossing Over $100m', for instance, went to *Twister* in 1996; 'Worst Reckless Disregard for Human Life and Public Property' was awarded to *Con Air* in 1997; and *The Cat in the Hat* won 'Worst Excuse for an Actual Movie' in 2003.

Paul Verhoeven, the Dutch director of *Showgirls,* was the first recipient to receive the Razzie in person at the awards ceremony in 1996. However, it is Tom Green, mastermind behind the movie *Freddy Got Fingered,* who in 2009 may be said to have most embraced the raucous spirit of the Razzies. A winner in a then unprecedented five categories ('Worst Actor/Director/Picture/Screen Couple/Screenplay'), Green is reported to have turned up with his own red carpet, which he unfurled heroically upon his arrival at the show. Apparently he later had to be dragged offstage due to his refusal to stop playing the harmonica.

THE TEEN CHOICE AWARDS

Every year a bunch of 13- to 19-year-olds vote on their cultural idols of the year. They then pile into the Gibson Amphitheatre in Universal City, California, and scream at them for something like three hours.

Winners (if there really are any in this scenario) are awarded custom-made surfboards. These are a nightmare to carry home, but they do offer protection against the howling hormonal mass that constitutes the audience. All of this is enough to make one wish that Mr Green would show up with his harmonica to lend a sense of dignity to the proceedings.

THE GUILD AWARDS

Each guild – the newly merged Screen Actors Guild and the American Federation of Television and Film Artists (SAG-AFTRA), Producers Guild of America, Writers Guild of America and the Directors Guild of America – also hosts its own awards ceremony every year. There may be more than those listed above, particularly as guilds periodically threaten to splinter, spin-off and re-form, but frankly our alleged expertise is in Hollywood, not industrial relations, and we don't want to bore you with any more than these.

The guild ceremonies are all clustered at the end of January and beginning of February in order to fit in before the big *kahuna*, the Oscars, which takes place at the end of February. These awards ceremonies offer excellent opportunities for bluffers, principally as the plethora of gongs given by organisations with abbreviated names allow you to make up your own.

The Bluffer's Guild Awards? Initiative, plasticine and gold spray are all you need to adorn your awards shelf handsomely with plenty of 'BGAs'.

ACCESSORIES OF SUCCESS

A shortcut to bluffing your way to success is bluffing *about* success. You need to know what successful Hollywooders splurge their cash on so you can give the impression of having made it in Hollywood – even if you don't have the money. Many of these items will strike you as unnecessary, frivolous and downright masochistic. That is their very point.

Nothing screams 'success' like the ability to spend money to make yourself miserable. True success in Hollywood is based on the large amounts you can blow on shrinks, divorces, and plastic surgery that makes you look like a Dalek.

ACUPUNCTURIST

Hollywood is chock-full of hypochondriacs, so it's not surprising that there is a thriving alternative medicine market there. At the top of this pyramid sits the acupuncturist. This is usually an older man of unclear origin who will have toured with at least one of the Beatles (normally Ringo).

Bluffers really need to know only two things about acupuncture: 1) it hurts a lot; and 2) it should not be attempted at home.

ART COLLECTION

If you are someone who has made serious money in Hollywood, you will no doubt have 'invested' some of it in art. This is one of the easier areas to bluff in, as arguably the whole concept of the contemporary art market is one massive con.

Do not despair if you can't afford to buy a Twombly, Kentridge or Baldessari. Nine times out of 10 you simply need to buy a large piece of white cardboard and scribble on it like a crazed five-year-old. If this looks like it isn't going to cut the mustard, buy a black-and-white photo and put a large, bright orange dot on it. You should then hang it somewhere very noticeable.

Advanced bluffers should graciously give away some of their original 'pieces' as evidence of their generosity and exquisite taste – and see if anyone notices that you whipped it up yourself in your garage. In two minutes.

Having an 'art collection' also allows you to hobnob with other collectors. Though the closest you may have come to owning an original painting is the one your six-year-old brought home from school, you should refer knowledgeably to your buying jaunts at Art Basel (in Switzerland, Miami and Hong Kong), the Frieze in London or the Armory Show in New York.

ART CONSULTANT

Art consultants are people who advise moguls on the best way to fritter away millions of dollars on questionable art. If you went to their homes, you would likely find reproductions of peaceful Impressionist haystacks and water lilies, rather than the monstrosities they advise their clients to buy. Art consultants have the great advantage of not having to put their own money where their mouth is or live with the stuff they tell other people to buy.

Bluffers who are finding it hard to fib about Hollywood might consider this as a secondary career, even if the closest they've come to the study of art history is watching Rolf Harris drawing cartoons on Sunday night television and asking 'Do you know what it is yet?'

CHARITY

Everyone in Hollywood has a charity, and we suggest you do too. It's not enough to make the odd donation now and again to the Salvation Army; in Hollywood, to fit in, you actually need to *invent* a charity. (We recommend anything to do with animals. Everyone loves them.)

Having a charity allows you to rub shoulders with the rich and famous and also covers a multitude of sins. You can be any of six kinds of scoundrel, but get yourself on the board of a charity and you are sainthood personified.

Very rich Hollywooders allow themselves to be 'honoured' by charities all the time, which basically means that they shake down their buddies to buy tables and art at a charity event while they receive some crystal piece of tat and are hailed as 'a great humanitarian' in front of an audience.

GOLD-DIGGER

The precursor to the trophy wife or husband. They can be as vicious as stage mothers. They're usually notoriously well put-together and exude an air of conspicuous consumption. They make frequent references to rich people they have dated, all of whom seem to have owned private planes, though they themselves drive a clapped-out Civic that they park round the corner on dates.

The nice ones are simply looking to build a better life for themselves and to have some fun while they do it; the mean ones are killers in training.

We would advise you to avoid gold-diggers at all costs. The good news is that they have an inbuilt sensor for cash and may already have sniffed you out as a bluffer, in which case they will simply ignore you.

TROPHY WIVES (AND HUSBANDS)

A trophy wife should ideally have three things going for her: an age of at least 25 years less than her husband, pneumatic breasts and no discernible interest in anything (except, of course, shopping). A trophy husband simply needs the ability to look masculine while carrying his wife's handbag. Trophies tend to be second or third spouses, as they will normally only latch on to someone who has already made money (and not lost too much of it in a divorce settlement).

We do not advise you to get involved with a trophy.

They are notoriously tricky to handle and their inane background chatter about tooth whitening, the Bar Method and Hermès bags may distract you from your bluffing. Rather, we suggest that whenever people ask about your marital status you make noises about Cindy/Fabrizio going away on a silent retreat/trip with the Buddhist guru/holiday with Ivana (Trump) and smile in a pained way.

Gold-diggers are notoriously well put-together and exude an air of conspicuous consumption... Avoid them at all costs.

CHEFS

It is not within the remit of the trophy wife or husband to cook, so a personal chef is a requirement for any self-respecting Hollywood bluffer. As you will avoid food with the fervour that a trophy spouse avoids paid employment, it does not really matter whether this person has any culinary aptitude; it is simply enough to have him or her hanging out in the kitchen wearing a white hat, banging saucepans around.

We suggest that bluffers of less substantial means merely tell people that they are 'off' eating. Some people in Hollywood have not had a sandwich in 20 years, so will be sympathetic.

HOUSEKEEPERS

Again, this is a holdover from the ornamental nature of the trophy spouse. He or she will be too 'busy' to clean the house, so you will have to get someone in.

Bluffers who expect company imminently, but lack the cash to hire help, should try to convince a gullible friend to don a black-and-white maid's outfit (not one from your local sex shop; we're not going for the saucy French maid look here). Alternatively, you can simply feign bemusement when confronted with household equipment. Stare distantly at the kettle as if you've never seen one before, while muttering about 'Rosa' being 'away for the week'.

FENG SHUI CONSULTANT

People with more money than sense (and this is most of Hollywood) are never far from a feng shui consultant. These characters are able to charge remarkable amounts of money to state the obvious, such as: 'Position furniture correctly' and 'Make repairs promptly'.

If you already know that it's not a good idea to put a massive sofa in the middle of a thoroughfare, or that you need to fix a leaky roof as soon as you can, you are qualified to be one of these overpaid mumbo jumboists – or at least to pretend to have employed one. For extra credit, festoon your bedsit with crystals and talk intensely about 'flow'.

NANNIES

You will be too busy bluffing your way around Hollywood to put up with your children, so you're going to need to pay someone to do this, too. The children never tend to belong to the trophy spouse so you can't really ask him or her to look after them. Besides, a trophy wife might decide to use them as trimming for one of her expensive coats.

PERSONAL TRAINERS

Despite the fact that many Hollywooders have avoided carbohydrates for 10 years, they still need a personal trainer to visit their house periodically and yell at them while making them do hundreds of burpees. Their clients may be incredibly powerful and aggressive in their day jobs, but leave them alone for 10 minutes with a trainer and they will be crying like a baby. Personal trainers are the Hollywood flagellants of the twenty-first century: constant reminders to its age-obsessed population that the ego is strong, but the flesh is weak.

Personal trainers come in a few categories: those who are good at their jobs, those who are actors and want to sleep with you for advancement, and those who are actors and want to sleep with the trophy spouse.

POOL BOY

If you don't have a pool, you should still consider hiring a pool boy. You are a bluffer, after all, and the lack of the very thing they are meant to clean should not stand in your way. If necessary, you should grandly show the prospective pool boy your bathtub, referring to it earnestly as a new kind of Scandinavian swimming exercise craze.

There are many pool boys who simply want to do a

good job and service your pool. Others are 20-something slackers whose greatest pleasure in life is wandering around rich people's backyards partially stoned and semi-naked, hoping to find sexual favour with one of the occupants. Gender preference is not generally an issue in these instances.

PRIVATE DETECTIVE

A great way of confirming that your paranoia isn't imaginary. Everyone *is* actually out to get you.

SECOND HOMES

Second homes are something any bluffer should be able to mention. You should frequently say that you are 'out of town' for the weekend – even if this means that you're just going to the nearest shopping mall.

PRIVATE JET

You'll need a private jet to fly to your second (third and fourth) home. The only real way to get around claiming to own a plane when you don't is to lie outright. A more devious approach is obviously preferable. For instance, speak of your neurotic (whenever you use this word a Hollywooder will nod in sympathy) fear of private planes since what happened to Auntie Grace over the Adirondacks. Dabbing your eyes with a tissue, you will say in trembling tones: 'I still haven't got over it, and I haven't been able to get in a Gulfstream since.'

LIMO COMPANY

All Hollywooders have a limo company on speed-dial. They use them for trips to awards shows, the airport, or simply to show they have money. You can arrange for a cut-price alternative by having your best mate borrow his dad's car and drive you around wearing gloves and a peaked hat. Ideally, you should sit in the back, wearing sunglasses with a copy of *Variety* ostentatiously displayed. (This will not work if his dad's car is an old Skoda.)

PLASTIC SURGERY

Consider this: people who have had plastic surgery are consummate liars. Similarly, the gentleman who tries to engage you in earnest conversation while sporting an ill-fitting toupee is a man who is not only lying to your face, but considers you a gullible idiot and is preying on your politeness not to expose him at any second by shouting: 'That isn't your real hair! Do you think my eyes don't work? I literally cannot take a word you're saying seriously, sir! Take that rug off your head and let's begin again!' (We share similar feelings about males who dye their hair: it is frankly one bluff too far.)

It is almost impossible to have a chat with anyone who has had 'work done' because you're forced to stare at their augmented body parts to ascertain what exactly has happened. This is unfortunately most pertinent for fake breasts, so your search for the truth rather unfairly results in you looking like a garden-variety pervert.

Rather than taking the usual Hollywood route of claiming

never to have had plastic surgery, instead audaciously bluff that you have had loads of work done. Your 'honesty' will be refreshing – particularly if you've never been anywhere near a scalpel. Claiming to have had plastic surgery when you haven't will allow you access to the rarified, affluent club of people so rich that they can afford to mutilate themselves. An added bonus is that it enables you to draw attention to your superior looks (even if they're not).

You should feel free to be specific about the parts of yourself you're pretending to have had modified with such comments as: 'You don't think nature would give me

Audaciously bluff that you have had loads of work done. Your 'honesty' will be refreshing.

such a perfect conk as this...' and, while gripping your breasts like over-ripe grapefruit, you might invite your audience to touch them saying, 'You're looking at a major investment here.' If possible, be specific about the price points involved, although caution is advised here lest you look like an overzealous market trader ('Got this lovely pair of coconuts for a fiver...', etc.).

SHRINK

With all the stress of the aforementioned acquisitions (or

of pretending to have them), you may well find yourself in need of some psychological TLC. Shrinks operate (very empathetically) on a sliding scale in Hollywood, so the first thing they will do is size up your bank balance, rather than your mental state, as you walk through the door.

We're not suggesting that you seek a therapist. After all, the fascinating, myriad mind of a bluffer is far too sophisticated for even the most brilliant psychologist to unravel.

There's no point in pretending that you know everything about Hollywood – nobody does – but if you've got this far and you've absorbed at least a modicum of the information and advice contained within these pages, then you will almost certainly know more than 99% of the rest of the human race about how Hollywood works, who the players are, how to become one, and how to survive the experience. What you now do with this information is up to you, but here's a suggestion: be confident about your new found knowledge, see how far it takes you, but above all have fun using it.

And watch your back at all times.

Think you're ready to make it in Hollywood? Check first with our quiz at bluffers.com.

GLOSSARY

ACE This refers to an honorary society of film editors (American Cinema Editors). It is included here because you have to admire anyone who prints these initials after their own name. They are truly of one mind with bluffers.

Alan Smithee The pseudonym used by directors who want to remove their name from a film. It's slightly like crashing your parents' car and saying someone else did it.

Apology Something very rarely heard in Hollywood. As the adage goes: 'Never apologise, never explain.' Useful, if slightly obnoxious advice for a bluffer.

Art house Cinema that exists solely for audiences to brag about their intellectual fortitude. Do not take a new date to an art-house flick if you want to get more than a hug later that night.

Ayem This is *Variety* slang for morning. It is a little annoying and may make you look illiterate should you use it in everyday correspondence.

Backdoor pilot Not what you might fear. This is a television episode that can function as a stand-alone piece or as the first episode of a series.

Bare-faced cheek Aka how to get ahead in Hollywood.

Bird Not one's wife, girlfriend or the well-endowed lady behind the bar at The Nag's Head. This means a satellite. Also used to describe a television channel broadcast by one.

Blacklist There was a dark time when Hollywood embargoed its own kind, accusing them of that most aberrant form of social behaviour: communism (other peccadilloes, such as being a snitch, seemed to pass without censure). The days of the blacklist are, thankfully, over. They have now been replaced by a system that is far more personal to its users: the s**tlist. If you've worked in Hollywood for more than a year you will have one. It is the only way to make it through the days of being abused, ignored and disparaged. Late at night, each assistant goes home and adds another name to the s**tlist of people they will revenge themselves upon when they are rich and powerful. Bluffers are advised to keep their own s**tlists; it doesn't matter if you haven't met the people featured on them.

Boffo *Variety* talk for 'outstanding'.

'Brave choice' How to refer to something you've royally cocked up.

Buddy How to refer to everyone in Hollywood. Particularly if they are not. 'Best buddy' is someone who has really given you the shaft. 'Baby' is a common alternative for the more patronising Hollywooder.

Casting couch Conventional way for a starlet to display her acting talents.

Come to Jesus An honest conversation. Very rarely occurs in Hollywood.

Coverage Getting someone else to read and summarise your scripts for you.

Creative differences When people can't get along and the more powerful one has the other sacked. We recommend this as a great way for bluffers to end relationships in any area of their lives. It adds a certain nobility in being dumped and sure beats being told, 'It's not you, it's me.'

Dating up, f*ing down** The traditional pattern for romantic relationships in Hollywood: you date people who are higher on the totem pole than you are, and sleep with people who are lower.

Development process A studio or network buys something. It then spend two years and millions of dollars trying to make it into something else, before reverting to the original idea and script (also known as 'development hell').

DVD A dying revenue source for the studios. The future is the internet, kids.

Exhaustion Spectacular and well-publicised drug problem.

Exhibitor Not the bloke who got arrested in the park for indecent exposure. An exhibitor is an organisation responsible for showing movies. A more straightforward word for this would be 'cinema'.

Favoured nations The guarantee that no one is being paid more than you are. It seems like a strangely socialist notion for a town such as Hollywood.

Foley/foley artist A guy in a dark room who makes his living recreating the 'clip-clopping' sound of a horse walking using only a pair of coconut shells.

Franchise The studio equivalent of legally printing money. Franchises are movie series that can be spun-off and rebooted endlessly in order to fill corporation coffers.

Green light When a script is ordered into production. This process is characterised by 'Go! Go! Go!' (followed by 'No! No! No!').

Happytown This is what Sammy Glick, the protagonist of Budd Schulberg's seminal novel *What Makes Sammy Run,* called Hollywood. It is heavy with irony.

Headshot The photograph actors use to convince people they are better-looking than they are. We advise bluffers always to have a few of these on hand to sign and distribute to unsuspecting passers-by.

Hyperbole The universal language of Hollywood.

'I loved it' Time-honoured way of telling creatives that their work is terrible. Shortly after you have heard this phrase, expect to be sacked.

'Let's do lunch' Translation: please, never call me again.

Leverage How much you can shaft someone and get away with it.

List As in 'You are definitely on the list'. Those seeking jobs view this as having their candidature confirmed. Instead, they should ask which list (*see* 'Blacklist', page 100).

Loyalty This word does not exist in Hollywood. Bluffers: please disregard.

Mercury poisoning *See* 'Exhaustion', page 101.

Mise en scène Trust the French to come up with a fancy-sounding phrase for something that's very simple. Refers to the elements making up a shot: set, actors, props, etc.

Money The fairy dust that makes Hollywood's wheels turn.

Mouse House The house that Mickey built (aka Disney).

Nielsen ratings This is the system for measuring television ratings in the USA. No one quite understands how it works. There are rumours of little black boxes in people's homes. Refer only vaguely to the ratings and manipulate them to suit your own ends. People make careers out of this in Hollywood.

Nut Operating expenses, money. Covering your nut is always advised.

OB/Outside broadcast This generally refers to news coverage that is shot outside the studio, commonly using one of those little vans with a satellite stuck on its top like a rogue cop surveillance van.

Opinion Never be afraid to have one in Hollywood. Particularly about a film or show you have never seen.

Original voice A gift that starts out as an asset in Hollywood and rapidly becomes a liability.

Pay or play The guarantee that even if you don't work on a show, you will get paid. This is something for all bluffers to aspire to. It is also known as 'easy money'.

Pilot The first episode of a television show. You should be careful when using this word around people who are not involved in the entertainment industry: a British director once told an immigration officer that he was visiting LA in order to 'shoot a pilot' and ended up in jail before his agent could explain the situation.

Power What Hollywood's all about, baby.

Prep/production/post **Prep** Where you anticipate the mistakes you will make. **Production** Where mistakes are made. **Post** Where you try and fix the mistakes.

Product placement Another way Hollywood sells its audiences more stuff. Some placements work seamlessly, others – well, not so much. One needs only think of the poor Coca-Cola executive who decided it was a good idea to team up with violent thriller *Natural Born Killers*.

Propaganda A form of film mostly favoured by autocrats. Usually with lots of singing and men marching in shiny boots and tight trousers.

Real World Something all Hollywooders and bluffers should avoid at all costs.

Recycling Hollywood is one of the most eco-friendly towns around. This is shown by the frequency with which they recycle their own ideas.

Runaway production Production that has decided that it is too expensive to shoot in Los Angeles and eloped somewhere with better tax credits (Albuquerque, Atlanta, New Orleans, Canada).

Shingle *Variety* speak for small business. Sounds a little like the word for grown-up chicken pox. Gross.

Sincerity Not one for bluffers to worry about in Hollywood.

Spec script Something a writer works on without having been commissioned in the hope that it will sell for megabucks one day. Arguably the first big spec-script sale was for *Butch Cassidy and the Sundance Kid*, which sold for $400,000 (£250,000) in 1967. Spec scripts can sell for as much as $5 million (£3,100,000) these days, although these are the exception rather than the rule. Novice writers are encouraged not to give up the day job just yet.

Stop-motion Animation that takes forever.

Studio accountant The only type of creative never to get sacked in Hollywood.

Team This is how actors, writers and directors refer to their representatives. What they may not realise is that the idea of team representation was invented by agents looking to pass the buck between each other.

Tenpercentery *Variety* lingo for agency.

Tent-pole A big movie. Normally released over the summer. Normally based on a franchise or a comic book. Normally makes millions.

Testing The process of screening a television show or movie to an audience of average Joes to tell a studio or network what they should think of it.

Topper Head of a company.

Tracking Research a studio uses to find out how well a film will do at the box office – and how many people may lose their jobs on Monday as a result.

Tyro *Variety* slang for someone new to a field.

Weekend read What all executives dread. On Friday they will take home 50 scripts. They will wake on Monday morning with their faces stuck to the paper and drool obscuring the words. Make your life easier: this book is all you need to read to ensure success in Hollywood.

'You've done it again!' Delighted exclamation you can pull out of the bag whenever you've had to endure a screening of a friend or colleague's terrible movie.

BLUFFING NOTES

Bluffing Notes

Bluffing Notes

Bluffing Notes

Bluffing Notes

Bluffing Notes

Bluffing Notes

Bluffing Notes

Bluffing Notes

Bluffing Notes

Bluffing Notes

Bluffing Notes

Bluffing Notes

Bluffing Notes

Bluffing Notes

Bluffing Notes

Bluffing Notes

Bluffing Notes

Bluffing Notes

Bluffing Notes

Bluffing Notes